Futuring

11 Steps to Purposeful Planning

James Davis

Printed in the United States of America

Published by Davis Publishing

ISBN- 978-0692392898

With honor and love, I dedicate this book to my wife,

Hytholine Davis. You have always been my biggest fan.

Thank you for always being in my corner.

Justin, Jocelyn, and Tynisha —I only desire the best for

you! I want to also want to say thank you to my siblings —

Jevon, Demetrea, Jarvis and Jermain.

Thank you…. To my father, Bishop James A. Davis Sr. and

my mother Doris Davis. Your support and prayers has

made me who I am today.

Table of Contents

Introduction

What is Futuring? Is it new age? Or some new abstract way of thinking? Initially, I had no idea. Three years ago, I was awakened in the middle of the night and this term consumed my spirit and my mind. I had never heard the term before, so I was interested in discovering if it was actually a word.

To my surprise, this was a business term defined by the definition which stated it was the field of using "a systematic process for thinking about, picturing possible outcomes, and planning for the future". I've always believed that a person's future was never a coincidence but a result of variables that were put in place to create an intentional outcome. As Christians, we are sometimes led to believe that we have no input as to our future and somehow we are just along for the "ride". But, I've come to discover that God will empower us with the wisdom, tools and relationships that will catapult our destiny at such an accelerated pace if only we would seek His way of doing things.

If we would put into operation and obey His direction for our lives, we can experience a life full of increase and fruitfulness, while still exemplifying a sense of holiness in our actions.

In this book, you will discover that God is not trying to keep anything from you, but wants to give you all that is rightfully yours through a strategic plan that brings increase to every aspect of your life.

Discovering Who You Are

I believe this is foundational for anyone who starts to inquire about the purpose of their existence. From a position of mental assent, we often think we know who we are because of the things we like and from observing our parental pedigree, ethnicity or cultural background. However, I believe to honestly explore this question, we have to lay aside our preconceived ideas and surface observations so that we can answer this by meaningful exploration and dialogue with God and sometimes ourselves.

I believe we must begin at the Garden of Eden. Genesis 2:7, *"And the Lord God formed man of the dust of the ground and breathed into his nostrils the breath of life; and man became a living soul"* (KJV). What God blew into dirt was His own spirit. His spirit in the Greek is the word "pneuma".

Man was created out of the Creator's very own Deoxyribonucleic Acid or what we know as DNA. This being could know, feel and process information at a level that would outpace any super computer of our day. And because Eden was not a place, but an environment, the atmosphere of the garden fed his intellectual ability that would supersede any modern scientist in academia. And because he intellectually operated as a "god" the Creator trusted him to designate the identity of every other creature that was in the garden. He didn't have to battle with his identity because the source of all he was existed in the Creator (Yaweh). Not only did man, whose name was Adam, personify the Creator, he was also given charge of the garden's preservation (Genesis 1:26). As the story goes on in Genesis we read the account of this "first man's" fall in Genesis 3:1-24. However, all of humanity was not eternally lost due to the "first Adam's" fall. For God our Father had a remedy in place for fallen men. Before the foundation of the world, there would be a "last Adam" (1 Corinthians 15:45). This "Adam" would relinquish His royal position in heaven, temporarily become both God and man in the earth, establish a new way of living, bare the penalty of sin, take authority over death, re-establish the garden of Eden in the hearts of men, and return to His throne in Heaven.

Now that we have established what God has done for us, it's time to embrace our identity and have the confidence to accept who we are. Because we have accepted Jesus and His Kingdom plan for our lives, we have access to the wisdom of God (1 Cor. 1:30) and supernatural knowledge. It's this character trait that makes us unique and different. Far too often instead of accepting our uniqueness, we allow others to define us. And because others have defined us, we give them space to manipulate us. But here is a question that may start the process of discovering you:

1. What would you pursue in life if you believed you couldn't fail? And why?

This is a very important question because the answer should drive you to a place spiritually, emotionally, and mentally. You see, you have only one life to live on this side of eternity. Very few people come back from the dead or a near death experience and is given another opportunity to live. Therefore pursuing who you are and being honest with yourself is important.

There are certain things about you that should give you a clue as to what God has created you to become. I'll use myself as an example:

1. I like to talk.
2. I like speaking before people.
3. I also like solving other people problems.

Now you notice every one of those statements started with "I". To some people that may seem arrogant. But I accept what I'm good and gifted at doing. I'm okay with complimenting myself.

The problem with most people is that they are gifted at doing certain things, but they are afraid to announce the gifts and talents that God has blessed them with because of the concern of what others will think of them. But, until you accept who you are and you become free from the opinions of people, you will always struggle with your identity because of what others think.

So because I have accepted those three statements I previously mentioned, I began to ask God to show me where and what field should I be involved in. And through a series of experiences, mentoring and training, I reached a place in my life where I'm operating in all three areas. Not only that, I'm also being financial compensated for my efforts.

Proverbs 18:16 states, *"A man's gift will make room for him and bring him before great men"*. You see, the area of your gifting is a clue as to where your identity is. And not only will your gift and talents create opportunity for you, people will pay you for your expertise. I'm convinced when people discover what God created them for, they will begin to live a life that is so satisfying and blessed. Because when you are walking in your identity, you can be yourself. You see, God created you on purpose and *with purpose*. There is a freedom that comes when you no longer have to be anyone other than yourself.

"The two most important days in your life is the day you were born and the day you found out why" – Mark Twain

Who Do I Need?

Proverbs 18:24 states, *"He that desires friends must show himself friendly"*. I honestly believe that no man is an island. You cannot make and fulfill your life's assignment without the assistance of people. However, let's be clear that being selective about your business and personal relationships is crucial and should not be taken lightly.

Once you have identified and settled on who you are, it's important to position yourself spiritually and professionally so that you attract individuals who are best suited to assist you in fulfilling your life's purpose. Far too often we make the mistake of immediately bringing people alongside of us that we are comfortable with, but have not fully taken the time to determine whether they are to be a part of the equation. I believe that you should prayerfully consider your business and personal relationships and take an honest assessment of what value the relationship adds to your life.

As Christians, we are called to love people as Jesus did and yet it's okay to set relational lines of demarcations. Jesus was our prime example of setting relational distinctions. While we see Jesus demonstrating love and compassion to the masses, he personally hand-picked twelve individuals to assist him in establishing a new living order called the Kingdom of God. So if Jesus could and needed to be selective, then it is essential that we intentionally and on purpose look to Holy Spirit and allow Him to assist us in building our pool of relationships. Furthermore, as we discover who should be in our pool of relationships, it is just as equally important that we identify who should *not*. Let's discuss who we should not be in relational alignment with as it relates to fulfilling purpose and destiny:

"The Parasite" – These individuals mean well, but often times will have all kinds of personal issues. They are looking for someone to make time and listen to the current "drama" that is happening in their lives. Initially, we are sympathetic and make ourselves available.

However, we soon discover that continuing conversations with these individuals is slowly "sucking" and draining our time, drive and motivation to accomplish other things. What has happened is that, in many cases, this person will not take responsibility for their own situational choices. And so they plant the burden of their situation into the lives of others and look for them to pray and provide them with solutions. One thing for sure is this; they are masters at taking up a lot of your time.

"The Critic" – These individuals don't necessarily mean to have a bad assessment of life or others, they just have a poor vision of anything that is good. Oftentimes, they have been raised and lived in a very judgmental environment, so therefore it is natural for them to offer unsolicited and often negative opinions about everything and anything.

The danger of having them in your personal and business inner circle is that they will constantly question your decisions and unintentionally promote an atmosphere of dis-unity among your other relational partners. They are so blind to the damage they cause, that they are convinced they are right and everyone else is wrong. In their own mind, their perspective on a situation is superior. If you have people in your life that are this way and refuse to make changes, my advice to you is to love them from a distance. See them for who they are and even be watchful of what they say about others. If you're not attentive they can even poison your heart against others who have not done you any harm.

"The Gamer" – These individuals are in your life to play "head games" and to promote their own personal agenda. They will tell you what you want to hear because they are creating a place in your mentality and carving out a place of influence in your life. The "Gamer" is never serious about your future. They are only interested in theirs and they feel that you would be the person to get their personal agenda accomplished. Their goal is to get you to doubt the validity of what God has called you to accomplish in life and somehow their idea will be best for you. However their idea really promotes them and not you.

Since we have mentioned who you shouldn't be in alignment with, let's discuss the kinds of individuals who you may need in your life:

"The Coach"- These individuals see your potential and are willing to push you to maximum performance. They are not intimidated by anything you have accomplished. They are willing to risk the friendship even if it means being brutally honest. You see, the "Coach" sometimes see in you what you may not always see in yourself. Their perspective about your capabilities is not clouded by your upbringing, pedigree, ethnicity or financial position. They only see your possibilities.

"The MVP" – These individuals play the game of life at a higher level than you. But's okay, because they are willing to show you how they accomplish what they do at a higher standard. I've personally sought out individuals that live at a higher level than me, so I could see an example of what was possible. For example, if you wanted to improve in a sport, you don't spend a lot of time practicing with people who play at your level because you have nothing to aspire to. But, if you desire to become better you find a "star" in that sport that plays at a higher level and then you have room to grow. Don't be the person who needs to improve but because of pride you refuse to acknowledge you need help. The "MVP's" that God brings into your life are there to help you become better at your craft. Your skill-set has to be constantly improving. As your skill-set is improving, you position yourself as a professional and your expertise can command better financial opportunities.

So, you see how important it is for you to identify who you need to help you accomplish your life's assignment. Don't take your business and personal relationships for granted. Don't assume that by doing nothing that the "right" people will just show up. You have to get serious about your future if you expect to see any kind of change.

It's better to hang out with people better than you. Pick out associates whose behavior is better than yours and you'll drift in that direction. – Warren Buffett

Who Do I Know?

This question will require you to take action. Personally for me, I had to take opportunities to get in the presence of people who could help me. I've learned to move away from people that have my problem and move towards those who had my solution. In my book, "Fulfilling Prophetic Destiny", I discussed how I relocated from Richmond, Virginia to Virginia Beach, Virginia and how certain geographical locations bring you into the company of different mind-sets. Now it's important to note, it's not enough for you to align yourself with individuals who have your answers, but you also must bring something into the relationship that is worth developing and promoting. Your gifting and talents may give you access to individuals who recognize your possibilities and favor you.

This is why it's important to refine and develop those talents and giftings because the abilities you possess will at some point open a door that leads you into the pathway of meeting others who have the influence and connections to promote you. If I was to put what I've just stated in a mathematical equation it would be like this:

Preparation + Opportunity = Success

So often we desire the opportunity, however when the opportunity avails itself, we are ill prepared for the encounter. This is why we must find ourselves in the company of those who can mentor and groom us for our "moment" in the spotlight. These individuals in many cases have the influence and experience to show us where the pitfalls are and can keep us from making business and personal disasters for ourselves.

Where do we find those individuals who can recognize what's in us and help sharpen our potential? You will have to move from your comfort zone and become connected with organizations and groups that foster those giftings and talents. For example, if you desire become a better speaker, then join an organization which specializes in public speaking and leadership skills. If acting is your talent, then become a part of a local theater or playhouse. My point is that your expertise and circumference of relationships will grow exponentially as you align yourself with those who are in a position to promote you. Finally, becoming a part of a larger organization that promotes your skill set forces you to make friends and become acquainted with other personality types that are different from yours.

These settings promote interaction and relationships that will help strengthen your own personality type. Also, the continuing interaction with others will give you the experience that is needed to make adjustments around other business and personal relationships that you may have.

If you want to be unique, hone your skills and expertise in an area that causes you to be noticed. Make it so, that you are so outstanding in your craft, that others are referring people to you. You will be so referred, there will be little self-promotion on your part because your specialization is now on a referral basis.

If everyone is moving forward together, then success takes care of itself.
- Henry Ford

What Should I Charge?

People pay for expertise. This is why certain occupations can command certain incomes. Why? Because the person has a skill set that is uncommon. Don't de-value your expertise by charging lower fees or commissions. Because of the time and effort that was put into your specialization, you have a right to be financially rewarded. There is a passage of scripture that says in Romans 12:3, *"that a man is not to think of himself more highly than he should"* which is correct, because we recognize our abilities to enhance the lives of others is a gift from God. But, the scripture <u>does not</u> say that we shouldn't *think high!* In other words, recognize that your expertise in an area should not be taken lightly. People have a tendency to respect a profession or service that has a value attached to it. Why? Because if you don't believe that what you do has value, why should they?

What price should you charge for your professional expertise? I believe you need to ask yourself a few questions and do research in order to answer this question.

Because of the internet, so much information can be captured with a few key strokes. Visit a few websites of individuals or organizations that are already involved in the same line of business. Even though technology is at our disposal, it never should replace a phone call or making a personal appointment to visit that business. Sometimes a personal and physical appointment may allow you to capture more information than you could if you had only made a phone call. This personal appearance may allow you to ask questions and meet decision makers who may be more open to share industry secrets because of a physical meeting compared to a conversation over the phone.

Also consider the location of your business. Geography has a significant impact on accounts receivables. Many factors such as local employment conditions, local competition, and current trends all have an impact on how you charge for your services. Finally, be flexible in the event you have to make adjustments in pricing. Sometimes be willing to negotiate on something now, only to obtain something better in the future. Keep in mind, whatever you charge in pricing, people must see the value in your services. If not, they will shop your competition.

If you create incredible value and information for others that can change their lives - and you always stay focused on that service - the financial success will follow. – Brendon Burchard

Where?

I have found this question can be a challenging question to answer. So many factors are involved in establishing a venture, business, church plant, etc. Never take the location of your establishment for granted. The idea that "if you build it, they will come" has proven over and over again that this is a false foundation to establish any entity on. We live in a society where people are busy. And often times they are looking for the path that is the shortest route with the least effort exerted. And if they have to go out of their way, wherever the destination is, it must be worth their drive.

If your establishment requires someone to physically make an effort to visit your place of business, you as the owner, entrepreneur or founder must research your location and the various pathways to get there. While we live by faith, you and I must understand that faith is educated. Faith factors in all the resources and obstacles and allows us to see wisdom through Holy Spirit.

Holy Spirit gives us supernatural insight as to where our location should be for the establishment. Wherever God has called you to be, He commits His power to help you get the location resolved.

Let's explore some practical things that are needed in order to finalize the physical location of the business you are called to establish? Keep in mind, this applies to all kinds of businesses and nonprofit entities. Here are some steps that need to be considered:

1. Will your business fit into the current zone category for the location? Or are there pending zoning changes?

2. Will you be on a main road or side street? What will be your street visibility?

3. If the current structure needs changing or additional space, have you checked into city/county permit requirements?

4. How much parking space will you have? This affects how motivated your customers, clients or parishioners will be when it comes to visiting your location.

There are several other considerations; however I wanted to give you an idea of the questions you need to consider. The location of your place of business is crucial. Where it is located affects "foot traffic" and parking. For example, if you have a facility that is being used as a church and if people are having difficulty finding a place to park, they will more than likely visit someplace else. It doesn't matter how blessed or "anointed" the services are, they will become frustrated in trying to locate a space to park. This in turn will motivate them to attend elsewhere for worship.

Address all location hindrances early in the process. Don't discount the validity of any barrier, because your customers won't. Don't make it easy for your competition to draw business away from your establishment. Your competition is hoping you are naïve as to what your customer base is experiencing.

The entrepreneur always searches for change, responds to it, and exploits it as an opportunity. – Peter Drucker

Money

What is money? A tool that provides options. Ecclesiastes 10:19b states, it *"answers all things"*. While money cannot replace the finished work of Jesus, it helps us to choose the quality of life that the Bible says we can have. Why is this topic of money so important in planning? Because it's availability helps us to determine future endeavors. The subject of money cannot be overlooked or belittled when it comes to future business, ministry and personal activities. For most endeavors the availability of financial resources is a key to determining not only the quality of our future accomplishments but also how long those endeavors can be sustained. This is why I believe before any business or personal projects are implemented it may be best to meet with a financial professional such as an accountant or a financial planner to carefully lay out a strategy.

Sometimes with all the details and planning that goes into a project or new venture, we may become blind to what's obvious because we are so emotionally attached to the project. With a second set of "professional eyes" there is an unbiased and objective perspective that is afforded to us. I believe, if we consult with Holy Spirit, He will lead us in the path of those who can help determine the path we should take while maximizing our dollars.

Why do I believe that accountants and professional financial planners should be consulted? Because they understand financial laws and can assist us with the documents that are needed to account for every dollar spent. These individuals can assist with financial projections and forecasting behaviors that help to determine future earnings. They can help to shape and give clear input on an entity's Profit and Loss Statement (P&L). What is a Profit and Loss Statement you may ask?

It is a financial statement which summarizes the revenues, cost, and expenses incurred during a specific period of time – usually during a fiscal quarter or year. Why is this document so necessary? In some cases in order to attract investors willing to provide financial capital (liquidated money), many may request to see a P&L statement. This helps to reassure the investors that they will or will not see a return on their investment.

It's really important that business owners, entrepreneurs or ministry leaders understand why this kind of document is so important. God desires that we are good stewards (caretakers) over the resources He has given to us. What better way to honor God with what we have than being able to give an account of our financial resources so that we in turn have thriving businesses and ministries.

While I understand there are still some churches who feel that business and there practices have no place in the local church, it is important that the local church has the financial tools that generate reports so that the leadership of the organization can objectively understand the financial health of the organization. Whether it's a secular business or church, both entities need money to operate and fulfill the purpose of their existence. In order for the business to be able to fully convince owners or investors that the finances are "sound" it takes this kind of report to convey that message.

A good financial plan is a road map that shows us exactly how the choices we make today will affect our future – Alexa Von Tobel

Learn the Language

Every industry and organization has its own language and acronyms that they use to communicate within their for-profit and non-profit culture. This language is developed over time through ideas, inventions, processes and procedures. It is imperative that anyone intending to become involved in any enterprise should learn the language of the chosen field or industry. It is through the knowledge of the terminology and acronyms of the chosen field that an individual becomes confident and builds an area of expertise. This is why, I often encourage individuals to learn as much of the companies language before the interview. In many cases during the interview you can demonstrate to the interviewer that you are serious about the opportunity because you have taken time to learn the language. You see whenever you learn a language, you are forced to learn the culture. When I speak of culture, I'm referring to its values, principles and beliefs. Much of an organization's language (terminology and acronyms) is birth from what it believes in.

I also believe understanding the language of an entrepreneurial pursuit, positions one within a company or spiritual arena with the confidence to have meaningful conversations with individuals already in that line of work and to even initiate dialogue. That may in turn create a relationship with that person simply because you both are speaking on the same terms. Finally, learning the language of your intended profession increases your vocabulary and presentation skills. You may be forced to use terminology that better addresses an area while developing the body language to accompany your presentation. People have a tendency to feel more confident with someone who has taken the time to perfect their message and uses their vast vocabulary to accurately convey thoughts.

More business is lost every year through neglect than through any other cause.
-Rose Kennedy

Internships

Often we think of an internship as a training period designed for a high school or college student that needs to get experience in order to hopefully acquire a future position with a company. But the job market today has forced many people to re-evaluate their skill-sets whether due to a past layoff, company downsize or simply their skill-set is being replaced by technology. These changes have forced individuals to take a second look at their career future.

Community colleges and technical schools are seeing a major increase in enrollment because people desire to be in more control of their future career endeavors. Internships are also allowing individuals who are willing sacrifice their free time to get hands on training. While many employers promote hiring someone with a post high school education, they still prefer an individual that has demonstrated actual work experience in that area along with the education.

Internships are also a great way of getting your hands "dirty" in a new field while building up your resume. It also gives you the opportunity to work alongside those who have an expertise in that area so that you can see the knowledge you have being applied to a real-life situation. I encourage every person not to let pride get in the way of pursuing an internship. If an entrepreneurial pursuit or career opportunity is what you desire, you don't have to quit your current employment or position. Just carve out some time and meet with someone in that desired field and ask them to allow you to intern with them. To your surprise, they may be willing to pay you for doing a part of the job they don't prefer and yet you are getting the experience that you need. Finally that internship will allow you to have another character reference that can be used to open up other doors of opportunity.

I'm sure you've heard the saying; "it's not what you know, but *who you know*". This person who you have interned with can personally acknowledge your ability to perform a service because they were responsible for your developed skill-set. Go ahead and seek out an internship. Even if it's unpaid opportunity, people will be impressed by your pursuit of their expertise.

"Don't be afraid to give up the good and go for the great." - Steve Prefontaine

"Grow the People...Grow the Organization"

While this is a profound statement, I cannot take credit for this; it goes to John Maxwell. However, I want to elaborate on this statement. As I look back at my years of experience as a Senior Pastor and my real estate business the one thing that I noticed is that businesses and churches that major in "growing people", found a greater amount of success and return on the investment they made in their leaders. Far too often these organizations are so focused on the bottom line financially that they forget, organizations and entities grow as a natural result of the people who make up these organizations. It is essential that business owners and spiritual leaders understand that all of the technology, tools and financial implementations mean little if your staff is not professionally developing in their current positions.

It is essential for you as an entrepreneur, business owner or spiritual leader to look for seminars and the financial resources to spend on your staff's education. Your business budget needs to accommodate training and continuing education for your staff. Because of the demonstration and concern that you have as a business owner or spiritual leader towards your staff's professional growth and development, you will further increase their loyalty to you and the organization.

As your business budget continues to accommodate training and continuing education for your staff, your staff will develop and grow and implement changes and processes that will take your organization to new heights. And let's not forget the boost in morale that comes as your staff and leaders feel and believe that the "heads" of the organization is seriously concerned about them.

Also, I believe the answer to incompetence is training and exposure. When I say exposure, I mean to new ideas and fresh perspectives. That might include seminars and workshops for your staff. Make it a part of the job description that your staff be available certain times of the year for these type of learning events. You can never spend too much money to overcome incompetence. Think about it like this, there are some business decisions that if made, will cost you more to rectify than it would have cost to send that individual to a class.

From a long term perspective, as your organization is growing, you will have a strong pool of individuals to consider for future promotions and expansions. Because you had previously invested in your staff and now as the owner or spiritual leader you have future leaders that are competent and able to take the organization to new levels.

You see, it doesn't matter what the current size of your organization is because it's not about where you are, but where you choose to be. So set a goal for your company or religious institution as to where you would want to be. Begin implementing training and tools to launch your dreams forward. Again, make it mandatory for your staff that certain classes and events are attended in order for future promotions. Before you realize it, growth, multiplication and increase is being experienced within your organization.

The growth and development of people is the highest calling of leadership.
– Harvey Firestone

Funding

One of the most common issues that entrepreneurs and new business owners have to consider is funding. New ventures have start-up cost. Depending on the business or religious pursuit, sometimes there's licensing, classes, and certifications. This is why it's important that before any new venture is implemented, questions, questions and more questions need to be answered and explored. In my book, Fulfilling Prophetic Destiny, I asked a series of questions that I feel are worth repeating. They are:

1. Why this business opportunity?

2. How much time are you willing to commit to the growth of your business?

3. How much money do you plan to make from this opportunity?

4. Will this opportunity draw money out of the

household budget?

5. If you are married, is your spouse financially supportive of this endeavor?

Why are these questions so important you may ask? Because for most start-up ventures, it may require financial resources that come personally from the owner(s). And those individuals have to initially balance the need of the new business and their personal expenses. And if there is a spouse, do they fully understand and are okay with financial resources that may have been set aside for future retirement and savings being diverted to fund a new business or spiritual endeavor.

The nature of the business may also dictate as to what pathway is best to secure funding. For example, if your endeavor is of a spiritual or religious nature, sometimes the organization that you are connected to may be willing to assist with the preliminary cost to establishing a place of worship.

For the secular business, many sources are available, such as your local Small Business Administration, government grants, taking out a second mortgage or bank loan. Whatever the endeavor is, there is money to get it off the ground. But you must be persistent and willing to pursue resources. Lastly, ask around. You won't be the first to have started a business from the ground floor. There are individuals and companies that will assist you with information, but you must pursue and make appointments to meet with individuals who can help point you in the right direction.

An entrepreneur without funding is a musician without an instrument – Robert A. Rice Jr.

9-5

While this book seems to address those who are self-employed or entrepreneurs, I understand there are those who work in the traditional job market and who are looking to break free from that day in and day out routine. Believe me, I understand completely. For a number of years I've always felt that a traditional 9-5 job really just didn't fit with my personal aspirations. I've always had the fortunate opportunity to acquire jobs that allowed me to maximize my gift of communication. Little did I know that these job opportunities were preparing me to pull away from the traditional routine of a work week and allow me to launch my future in a career field where I had natural abilities.

I often say to those who are looking to break free from being an employee to more of being their own boss, must understand that this should be done with much thought, prayer and good advice from those who have already taken that leap of faith.

What observations should one take notice about themselves before transitioning from a W-2 person to a 1099 person (self-employed)? I believe it starts with your natural abilities. You see, what you are naturally good at is your foundational asset. For me, I was comfortable meeting new people and being in sales. Anything I truly believed in, I had the confidence to promote and communicate to listeners that what I was selling, they needed. This was my foundational asset. Your foundational asset is something that you didn't have training in. You naturally just operate in this area and can see results. So what is your foundational asset? Secondly, while you are currently working a traditional work week, are you willing to spend time after work meeting with someone or spending time "shadowing" someone else? It also might mean taking a part time job in that area so you can get the confidence and experience to transition. Thirdly, are you willing to make a mental shift from a weekly or biweekly mindset?

When you become a 1099 individual or what we call an independent contractor, your compensation may not initially resemble what you were used to. But, this is where you embrace that you are no longer an employee, but an independent contractor. One of the benefits of being in business for self is that you have the potential to create a lifestyle with unlimited income potential. Here's how someone explained it to me years ago "You eat what you can slay". While I understand, it can be unnerving to go into a field where your paycheck is not limited to a particular time of the month. Understand, under this system you can get compensated for your efforts anytime of the month. Your plans are not dictated alone by the 1st or the 15th of the month.

Also you will soon discover that individuals that thrive as an independent contractor have the potential to earn a considerable amount of income compared to an individual who works the traditional 9-5 job. Why? Because, you are not limited and restricted to earn a certain salary or wage per hour.

It certainly would not hurt to have a savings or "nest egg" to draw from for those first couple of weeks in your new venture. Speak with individuals who have made that transition into the business you want to go in. Ask them about their transition. Learn what strategies they had put in place to make the cross over from being an employee to an independent contractor. Ask them about their challenges, the highs and lows, and even any regrets. Finally ask them; knowing what they know now, what would they have done different? You see, you don't have to reinvent the wheel. Others have already gone before you and paved the way. By going this route you save yourself a lot of time and resources. You will also learn from the mistakes and successes of others and watch your business and spiritual endeavors flourish.

This chapter was not written to belittle those who work the traditional work routines whether it's blue-collar or white-collar. I have worked in both. However, if you decide that you like the assurance and stability of a blue- collar or white-collar atmosphere, you should at least have a plan that enables you to periodically get promoted in that line of work. So, I suggest that if you are reading this book and this is where you are, here's the good news, you can move forward. How would a person move forward in an hourly-wage or even clerical position?

1. Education – enroll in a community college, 4 year degree program or just take some classes. Consult your employer about school reimbursement or tuition assistance. Some companies will assist in those areas especially if the classes are industry related.

Unfortunately, a high school diploma does not scratch the surface for getting better career opportunities. Because of technology in so many fields, even four year college graduates and individuals with graduate degrees may find it a challenge to land a position in their field.

2. Locate a career path that requires a specialized license, such as insurance agent, real estate agent, cosmetologist, etc. While these fields may not require a formal education from a community college, they all require a series of classes required usually by a local state board or municipality. Also, in many cases in order for that individual to maintain their license, they must periodically take continuing education in that field so that they may stay abreast of new changes and policies in that line of work. What's great about having a license in a specialized field?

You may be able to exempt yourself from certain rules or policies that you don't agree with by a particular employer. Because your license gives you the flexible to pick who you want to work for in that line of work. In other words, you don't have to limit yourself because your license gives you options.

Whether a 9-5 job or being self-employed, now is the time to plan for a bold move as far as your future is concerned. Pray and seek counsel regarding your future endeavors. Don't leave your future to chance and thinking that you will just fall into an opportunity. You must be intentional in your effort and your efforts will bring opportunity across your path.

From an early age I didn't buy into the value systems of working hard in a nine-to-five job. I thought creativity, friendship and loyalty and pushing the boundaries of what was acceptable was much more interesting. -Adam Clayton

You're only a decision away from a change....

Congratulations for completing this book, however. I must say, to really apply what you've read and have the wisdom to follow through; you must accept Jesus as your Savior and Lord of your life. If you really want to see a difference in your life, repeat this prayer of salvation:

"Lord Jesus, I want a fresh start in life. I understand you died for me and rose again so I can experience a good life. I surrender my will and my life to you. Thank you for accepting me. Thank you for changing my life and I look forward to the rest of my life being the best of my life. In Jesus name, Amen!!

Praise God, Romans 10:9:10 is the foundational proof that you are now saved. Now I encourage you to attend and get involved in a good Bible base - Word filled church and watch your life grow by leaps and bounds. God bless you!

About the Author...

James Davis attended Virginia Commonwealth University. After an encounter with God concerning his destiny, he decided to attend Bible College and received his Doctorate of Divinity from The Redeem Bible Institute. Dr. Davis, who also is a musician and singer, has dedicated his gifts unto the Lord. Dr. Davis travels and speaks in various churches and business events. His business acumen has allowed him to have an exceptional real estate business and he uses that success to motivate others to pursue their entrepreneurial dreams and make the most of their career. His insight along with exceptional communication skills, makes him a sought after speaker for your event. Dr. Davis serves as the Senior Pastor of Life Unlimited Empowerment Center.

For speaking and bookings:
James Davis
P.O. Box 61573
Virginia Beach, Virginia 23466
pastorjdavis@lifeunlimitedvabeach.org
www.lifeunlimitedvabeach.org

Books written by James Davis….

1. Fufilling Prophetic Destiny

2. Futuring - 11 Steps of Purposeful Planning